The Agency of Wind

The Agency of Wind

Laynie Browne

Avec Books

Grateful acknowledgment to the editors of the following journals, where excerpts from this book have appeared: *Art Access, Rhizome, The Poetry Project Newsletter, Torque* and *Talisman*.

"The Sweepress" was published as a section of *re: chapbook # 3*.

"The Bank of Common Knowledge" first appeared in *An Avec Sampler, 1997*.

Special thanks to Brad Davidson, Stacy Doris, Sarah Getz and Andy Levy for their early readings of this manuscript.

This book was funded by a generous grant from the California Arts Council, a state agency.

ISBN: 1-880713-12-8

Library of Congress Catalogue
Card Number: 97-78267

© 1999 by Laynie Browne

First Edition

All Rights Reserved.

Avec Books
P.O. Box 1059
Penngrove, CA 94951

for Brad Davidson

Contents

A Future of Mandolins: A Prologue	11

○

Windmills	15
Crane and Girl	19
The Windmaker's Door	29
The Tiara of Citronella (A Ballroom Criminal)	37
The Bank of Common Knowledge	51
The Sweepress	59
The Shepherdess of Land	71
The Sleep of Lamps	87
Hands Made of Mercury	97
A Girl in The Woods	107

○

Epilogue and Prologue	125

"Would now the wind had but a body: but all the things that most exasperate and outrage mortal man, all these things are bodiless, but only bodiless as objects, not as agents."

—Herman Melville

A Future of Mandolins: A Prologue

I am traveling on a gold cloud.
Where come and go no ships or ships logs
Those books of orchards borrow my mind

I mention all of the travels made of bells since it is seemly within these etchings which we traced upon the ground before setting out- consoled by keeping ships nearby of twilight.

Adrift, a tall thirst.
I carved my tongue.

Calm kind of strokes where we kindle an ocean awash.
Candles are wilted and shells wear their skeletons.

I refer to those who trudge, conjecturing the last appearances of a tower.

Windmills

I approached a windmill, but it was really a series of persons extending their limbs in a similar motion. As I approached they continued.

Is this the spot, I asked, where wind begins?

No, I was told, here wind is graduated.

Then, where is it begun?

We've only been standing here, moving our arms in a similar motion.

And which way would I walk across a hurricane in order to arrive at the next season?

Crane and Girl

> "... and Pelican Argo herself, who was chafing to be off, cried out, for she carried a sacred beam from the Dodoian oak which Athene had fitted in the middle of her stem. So they followed one another to the rowing benches and taking their allotted places sat down in proper order with their equipment by them."
>
> —Apollonius of Rhodes

The ages of mosses are not easy to guess, as the gesture which makes no movement, but draws nearer, silently rowing.

Each time the lily was to bloom upon water, a trip was expected, so that the crane never learned the color of the flower so carefully coaxed,

until once, the flower waited.

The predisposition of the flower in color was unknown.

This waiting was unexpected, as an underwater current, as not knowing the presence of water below where they sat.

A conversation ran on, as it appeared to onlookers.
The colors of such waters remain unknown.

Excuse me, begged the crane, but must I remove my
    headdress in your presence?

Of course not, answered the girl, because you
    mistakenly refer to your head.

In that case, continued the crane, may I have the
    honor, in your presence, of becoming headless?

The girl responds, and if we are all to do likewise, a
    flower would need no longer wait.
A conversation could run on.

in which case the headdresses were thrown.

Of certain storms and chemistries, there is no sense to suppose. I learned somewhat to ask, but that smaller, unanswered chime echoed through a gridwork unassailable. Light retracts within a pupil and then follows a treacherous path. You are less responsible for your token selves. This is how the mind goes into the day.

Please explain that statement, said the crane, motioning backwards—as they traveled away.

In their flight

the girl's lips

could only manage

entanglement

This is how the storm goes into supposing.

Who were you then, asked the crane. A corymb. The girl had no reply. A yielding hand in a game. Who were you then asked the girl. A black band worn upon hat or sleeve. A large wading bird with long legs, bill and neck. From the crinkled lobes of the corolla, a homonym, or mistflower. And who were you then asked the girl, this time impatiently. A cormorant, a sign of mourning. A female child, answered the crane, full of bends and turning. I was a marsh bird, replied the girl, mistress of the night flying moths, dwelling amongst papyrus. An heiress presumptive to a small opening in a rockface. While I hold these disguises, with which wing to winnow the waters. With which painting of a night scene to wake a fictitious force used to describe motion.

GIRL:

You have an idea of yourself upon rising, amidst many other ideas of yourself, and as you lift up your morning, so do you lift up all of the ideas of yourself lifting the morning, so that if you could watch a film of yourself, you might see one-hundred and eight images of yourself, lifting the morning.

CRANE:

And then am I less responsible for those one-hundred and seven that set forth into the day? It would indeed be very crowded in my nest.

GIRL:

Though all of my tools may be deliberately blunted, hand-mills coax a stream to sleep. Spiders are guards entitled to their positions, so as to set spirit traps. Though all of my tools may be late blooming geums, gales will soon cease. Of certain storms and tools, those notions which fill a nest, there is no sense to suppose. Waiting is unexpected, equal to wandering. This is how light may answer a gridwork, how a chime becomes a stream.

I rouse my bobbin

upon the streetcar

light, is but a drawbridge

The Windmaker's Door

A scent never remembered in sleep

A rain lost in white water

Walk forward and add the effects of trees

Vying pandemonium was found here, carved here

Which way to the windmaker's door?

If you want to know that you'll have to ask the doormaker.

And where is the spot where trees were carved?

A door only remembered in sleep.

The doormaker's door was encrusted with iron buckles and made of a very heavy wood. There was a knocker on which was engraved, "Behind this wooden facade lies my privacy." And, below that, a small metal plate contained the following information. "To order a door, please include the dimensions and materials you desire. Place note in slot 'D.'" I wondered at this for some time, and then, hesitantly wrote the following note and slipped it into a different unmarked slot:

"Can you tell me the way to wind's door? I speak as an empty sail."

I waited quite some time, and had nearly fallen asleep with my head against slot "D" when I received the following reply:

"What manner of being would ask such a question I cannot imagine. It is common knowledge that many living things require no door, nor doorstep."

What manner of being is required in order to imagine an invisible culprit, a worthy inhabitant in a weather of doors?

This location appears to be a sleep in echoing water. The diagram of a shelter made of glass and sails.

I walked discouraged, following my feet with no sense of direction, until I came almost suddenly to the edge of a cliff. Small solace. A wind plain. If you sweep down upon me, it may be that all of my questions are swept over this chasm, and that I may never find them again. It may be that I would be better off not to find them. But I think of them as if they were children, and would not like to imagine them at the bottom of blue rocks, with no guardian, so small and indistinguishable from gravel.

The wind spoke in bellows, and whistles. So small, with no guardian, indistinguishable from blue rocks, I stood fingering over and over again the small note from the doormaker. A question, a living thing, may change of it's own accord. "It is common knowledge that many living things require no guardian, nor distinguishing characteristics." If certainty is a point on a line, that remains unnamed, then wind is every point on the same plain, and behind this plain is another identical image.

The Tiara of Citronella
(A Ballroom Criminal)

"The Queen called me to her office. She was watering the flowers woven into the carpet."

—Leonora Carrington

I sat on a rose couch and drank rosebud tea. At first I said I wanted to sit on the rose couch, but then it was suggested to me that there was more than one rose couch. We asked the waiter to dry one off and pull out it's thorns so that we could sit more comfortably. There was a loud poodle, or a child crying. I turned my head quickly and caught my own startled expression. I had nearly collided with a mirror. As we sat this morning, Citronella implored me not to work. How to live on nothing? Since she did not consider this a significant problem, even worth addressing, I let it fall from my shoulders for the moment, although it did smother the napkin and leave an odd stain on the cloth. "You could say something, *fell through*," she offered. We asked the waiter to let down the umbrella so as to receive more sunlight. Late April sunlight, the first of its kind. And then, for the third time, she poured her newly filled cup of coffee into the treewell beside our rose couch, and got up for more. "Cold," she said, "it is absurdly cold." The tree responded by sending small leaf buds shimmying down onto our plates.

The house reeked of revenge.

The order of things was, get new glass cut.

The order of things was, come, you shall get new glass cut, in order to frame the girl standing in the clearing between- Come you shall know the history of the house. The order of things must never be changed. This is a challenge to all persons entering history.

Stop, the man was told, you are now tampering with breakable edges.

He was simply setting out across a territory known as gray glass. He set out at the clearing between. He set out from the house. Come, we will fling the order of things.

He set out across a lawn in the order of things prescribed.

And I wear this ring upon my finger in order to remember the circling effects of time.

And I wear this glass house in order to gaze upon the reflections of dawn.

And I wear this bracelet about my wrist in order to remember that I must set out tomorrow across such territory.

And I wear this cord about my waist so that you may lift me up from the stream. And I wear this cord around my ankle so that I may be saved from unnecessary catastrophes.

He set out to remove all compromises. He set out to compel audiences.

He set out among persons entering history.

My wrist set out.

The dawn set out.

A house set out, though I have seen no house.

His name set out across territories in order to compel an ankle, that you may lift me up from the stream, and catastrophes.

That was the way with the myth, and so his wrist remained unprotected.

I wear this tiara so that I may be sighted from a distance. I have covered my car with rhinestones, though I have no car.

And this headdress may come to represent visibility. And this myth remained propagated among stream people, and those inhabitants of the glass houses of history.

You may hurl an accusation, a monstrosity, you may shatter those who wish to set out, and then you must take it upon yourself, though to compel an ankle.

His name set out across several sheets of paper, envelopes, and touched the mailcarrier's elbow, slept within a vehicle, a box, another vehicle, and was never actually seen by him, but was assumed to have arrived within a particular region where his name was seen by various other eyes who paid it no particular attention.

An emerald mask makes an asset of time, so said Citronella to the star of the meeting opera. She took off the mask as she said so. On this side of the balcony, a rivet steers a school of bottlenecked fish and safety pin covered infants to their seats in the mezzanine. The riveted caretaker had bullet eyes and a barrel nose.

The cinder she had been so famous for tending within her mind had here escaped, and so she set out in search of the sparkling glass-gold.

Go into the region of many fountains, a referendum. Go covered in gauze. These are rules she did not gage. Eyes full of rain.

Good luck, whispered the gold pump.

The sky was dust from pearl and reddish stone. All things elusive as a single sunbeam.

Observations of a sundial:

My poor child, where will you lay your head?

A diadem lies close to her charm. She was carrying cartridges of dried pigeon plumage. "Poof"—and a horse emerged from her powders. Petals were strewn as she excited the observatory.

He has awakened early with the thought of a certain seal colored purse an old woman was carrying like bait with a certain swing switching. Between dances in lines, wearing masks and sipping a burgundy liquid, where gloves were considered to be marks of character, and carefully doubled to cover fingerprints. He is a diligent and cunning thief, spurring on others with his witty depths. The thought of a certain seal colored smile. He does not disappear from the text, but skims along the edges, where one dare not stop reading within the main borders in order to note his progress along a novel's edges.

Thief:

I wear these gloves, so that I may erase my identity, and protect those who would be harmed by the knowledge of my touch.

Her will was being fed by a doll who would not speak or listen. She placed her tiara upon the bedside and lay down. When she awoke the doll was upon her head and the tiara was nowhere to be seen.

Go and find your headpiece, ordered the doll.

The tiara set out.

The tiara was seen by many and interpreted by some individuals in the following terms:

The sight of setting stones is similar to night.

She wears a trap for light, where it may perish.

An unmistakable brilliance may dazzle.

And perhaps it may fall from her head.

There is no subject wearing an object, but an object walking.

There is only a remote possibility of finding similar matching jewelry.

I wear this ring around my toe in order to keep warm.

I wear this ring in my navel in order to ornament my beginnings.

There is only a remote possibility that you will find a matching head. There is only a remote possibility of keeping warm by falling. I wear this object walking in order to ornament all undertakings.

I wear this electronic device in order that I may never be asked to answer a telephone. I wear this subject so that I will not be mistaken for jewelry.

The tiara traveled, despite claims against her, such as gaudiness, irritability, and blinding brilliance. There is only a remote possibility that she will not reach her destination, or that she shall know it before she has stopped.

He set out across remote possibility to find a matching subject, in order to determine the nature of his undertakings.

I wear this destination as an undertaking, so that I may remember to ornament all undertakings.

He set out to discover the laws of ornamentation.

The tiara twice escaped from prison and bank vaults and continued on its way. The thief spoke, "so that I may remember to ornament all undertakings." All suspects set out to remember the law. All laws set out to become brilliant caretakers of the misbegotten, ill-fated.

All criminals in the region were asked if they would please set out towards their crimes at an earlier hour so as to permit subterranean traffic to hasten.

The thief spoke, "So that I may remember to rise at an earlier hour, I wear this electronic device across my chest."

So as to become foolproof, the tiara pulled out each of her stones, and replaced them with roadside flowers. Thus, transformed into a geometric bouquet, she traveled the countryside without much notice.

The Bank of Common Knowledge

I began to compose a letter in my head. It began, "dear squirrel," but I was interrupted by the woman who called me "dear." She was saying,

We work by basis of contribution, and drawing upon the common bank. In order to begin, you must first make a deposit. Our minimum is one hundred. I looked up and saw a sign above my head.

The Bank of Common Knowledge

She said, there is also the small matter of fees. I had no money, but since she said it was a "small" matter I decided to say nothing. Alright, I said, may I have some paper, and I will begin. I sat in a corner at a small table with a miniature pencil, next to a female alligator who appeared to be flustered. She kept sighing and panting, and sliding her scales on her table which made a most unpleasant noise. I tried to ignore her, although I could not help but to sympathize with her predicament. My list began with the following:

It is common knowledge that many living things require no door, nor doorstep.

It is common knowledge that many living things require no guardian, nor distinguishing characteristics.

It is common knowledge that the wind has no door.

It is common knowledge that windmills are actually persons with very strong arms.

It is common knowledge that this alligator beside me is having difficulties.

It is common knowledge that questions cannot be left behind; they cling most unkindly, but as they are innocent as children, one must take them along.

I had gotten this far when the alligator beside me got up noisily and lumbered away, knocking this and that with her tail as she went. She must have stuck her snout over my shoulder and was reading my list when she came to item five, and took it personally. I did feel annoyed, since those with snouts really shouldn't snoop. I was just adding this to my list:

It is common knowledge that those with snouts really shouldn't snoop.

when the "dear" lady came over to see what progress I was making. Her face made a variety of expressions while she read so that it was difficult to tell whether she was pleased.

Well, she began, I am personally much obliged to you for encouraging Alexandra to leave us.

Alexandra, I asked.

Yes, the alligator. You see, we find it most inappropriate to house reptiles.

But why, I asked, discriminate on the basis of blood temperature?

We are much indebted to you, she replied, ignoring my question, and on this basis we will accept your application. You need go no further.

Her cruelty was simply too much to bear. I thought of Alexandra and stood to leave, but then I decided to make an inquiry first, and resumed my seat.

I am most interested to know, has a crane passed this way recently, or a doormaker?

Certainly not!

Just then the walls began to creak, as if a storm were approaching. I could have sworn I saw the distinct outline of a crab within her right pupil.

Perhaps the wind has kept them away, I wondered aloud. At this comment of mine, her complexion noticeably colored.

She spoke in some temper: It is common knowledge that the wind is a very impatient and flighty entity. The last time the wind came through our office it took us quite some time to recover.

I was taken aback by the change in her manner. She looked around herself at the voluminous books fastened upon the walls with claws. It became clear that she had been all the while attempting to compose her features, searching for an appropriate thing to say. When she had accomplished her task she returned her gaze to me and spoke again.

I'm sorry, she replied, but we cannot accept your application.

Knowing my place exactly, and what I must do, I answered with all the seriousness I could summon:

That is most unfortunate, since I am not at present accepting refusals.

She made no reply. Her crab pupil scuttered, as if to follow me to the door. But she hastily closed her lid and clasped her hand over it firmly.

As I walked away the bank seemed to gleam like one copper coin being dropped. The sight was so clear in my mind I had but to turn around just in time to see a pig who was so large, that it's hoof could easily hold the entire bank of common knowledge. The pig lifted the bank, looked quickly around, and then swiftly dropped it through a large slit in its back. This accomplished, the pig ran into the distance, creating a large amount of dust as it went. The last I saw was the flourish of its curly tail at the horizon. The ground was shaking. I sat down to recover my balance. I thought of the "dear" woman. No doubt she would not have many applicants to turn away now. Thank goodness Alexandra and I had not remained within its premises. There was a big crack in the earth in front of me that must have opened up during the giant pig's departure. I was still clutching my list of items of common knowledge

It is common knowledge that the "dear" woman was never "dear."

I threw the list into the crack and rose to my knees.

The Sweepress

Veins are known to shiver, quest or quake. If I beckon a parlor door, I may vanish like a pebble in a well. The cabinet is in the sink. My fingers are on the dresser. A click is the door. When assaulted on all sides, a picture looks square. An ill wall, a borrowed brook, a broken answer. Longitude and laterwise.

Air in natural motion, as along the earth's surface, is only visible in relation to the figures it sweeps.

I am told, you must construct the future of mandolins.

Carry the heaviest paper you can find, and make a shelter.

So I am told, you weigh nothing, you walk the moon. Go and get some beggar grass. Then all of the stones will whisper in agreement.

So I am told, there is no glass to see through our fears. Here is a diagram of your geology.

 Walk into a mirror accordingly.

This location appears to be the tip of a gem. Walking, the beauty is all below, and feet are chiseled bone, splintered diadems. Where morning was, has moved. The length of one's hair will accomplish little (much shoepolishing). Walk the soldier lengths, and comb brows to follow clouds. A myriad of spools. I walk on silken spurs, mining for a scent.

The ordinary pathways we walk have lost themselves. There was no undernetting. A steel blade in a velvet scabbard. A race of meekless spiders. I am influenced by ages of silt which write sparse jewels. Everything else is the kind of water we seldom visit. A white pigeon against a white sky.

A day received is a day undone. Reindeer were once thought of as work animals. There is a kernel of mazy bat dances curtained by a sleeping soul. So I am told, if you set your bonnet right there is no longer dark laughter. I fill an oaken bucket, though this is no vouchsafe.

No treasure trove compares to nimble fingers. Even the threadbare, fain to shrink, when possessed by the east wind, walk with their gold-headed canes. The gist of this storm demon is a chimney corner glow. The rustle of steadfast testimony has no scowl.

As I stood on a threshold, the empress tree cast me a look with seed eyes. A symphony of violets, and a necklace of woes.

I am sorry for stealing the head glot of wine, the stickly skirt on the sticky ring.

she cries upon a winter porch

Remember those things you must complete as admonitions: spoke the spot of dust. She sat mopping soup from a floor less partial to polishing.

As I become this morsel of light, I lay myself down that I might find reflections within the tiles. She pressed her cheek to the floor and felt the ridges.

Trying to understand someone else's project of finery, she has a glimpse of the edges of dark shoes, polished to obsidians, and the ankles bearing prudence, sheathed within those opaque veils which suggest curtains. The sound of her steps staccato. In all of a flutter she is up from her perch, where she has not ceased confiding to the tiles all of her bewilderment. Her wrinkled brimming edges are frayed. A shrugging lily, swelling with the volatile rendering of observations which hinder her perception of householding.

For who is it she asks, if not I, who will have the tiles remain in their places so that while she walks across the floor they do not revolt and send her as they might, to her resting place. The bold insistence upon reverie is broken up into shards so many times within a moment that her recursive notions follow the course of a broom, and the eyes which darting across a dark hall, may search for any signs of vanishing gloss. Where the tiles have lost their luster, and the hearth has been filled with ash, this eye rests for an instant. The ankles look displeased as they have carried her to this deluge.

For who is it, she asks, if not I, who will allow those steps to continue plundering within their obsidian depths, and all of those treasures which need to be tended. For who is it, if not I, who will console the tiles at her passing. The true value I must assess as I trace those hairline cracks upon their surface circles and triangles. They travel of their own accord, just as those ankles, and as I at times may wish to move beyond the shards of fragmentation and wander far away from this intimacy with terra cotta.

The many tributaries I suppose can be waved as the outlines of coastline I have not ventured to visit, and the sharper angles, those borders of states drawn hastily. The small cracks between, where time has gathered is the antique finish my hands may not provide or erase, as those large bureaus which loom in their dark fathoms of history, valued as such.

The sleeping sense of all I have not touched surrounds me here in small relief. My world has descended beyond the line of shins and blocked outlines, as persons passing appear larger from this plane, the ceiling more expansive. When I stand at a window and lapse beyond the boundaries of these doorframes and fittings there is an obsidian night whose visitations are much larger than ankles and bureaus. And that I may wish to call upon those tracings which appear above seems little different, if only I am hindered by time, for it seems as soon as I have reached a tributary of stars, then the dark begins to fade and vanish at my touch, though it has taken all of my powers of concentration to reach the milky flourish through the telescope of my fingers extending out before me in a never ending chain.

So I am told, there are no visitations, only night and day as divided by a perpetual turning. So I am told, one may not reach with concentration very far into the atmosphere.

So I am told, only rain is condensation carried by those shadows that travel above the land, and no more prisms or laden jewels which disappear in wetness when pierced by a blade of grass.

Beyond those tapestries looking up through skeletons of trees are tracings whose centers do not grow dim and deflate as mere icons of necessity, but continue to travel of their own accord within my maps of visiting patterns.

The Shepherdess of Land

In a time of sanctuary all rivers belong to one family
Ash turns to primrose, taboo is made charm

No stake is cast out, no beast driven from pasture
I have not obscured a blue sea-plain, wide of fin

A threshold is a matter of robes thrown to sea

miasma, a crossing

For what reasons you have come
was never asked of a mountain

or the seed of rice enclosed within the paleae
smoke colored, identical with wind.

It took them one day to remove the floor; from there they dropped to their knees and listened. At which point they decided to dismantle the rest of the house.

Our house now has walls which wind constructs, spoke the child. And yet it is cold, replied her parents. I will retreat, she continued, heading over the nearest hill, and disappearing beyond a ridge.

And where will she go, asked the parents? I will go to the houses of water. But these houses have no walls, the mother answered. Yes, and even better, replied the daughter, no floor, and no canopy to cover the evening sky.

The dog as the bringer of fire.

The dog concluded: *If I shall not speak, I will not be a messenger.*

I approached a river, but it was really a series of swimmers extending their limbs in a similar manner.

And which way would I walk across this house, in order to arrive at the next?

My speech slid across the surface of paddles.

Somnolent voices   tumbled

in waves across the banks.

Would that this river had a body, which could be crossed.

Would that this dream contained the house you have summoned.

And the river swam away.

It would take a house with walls of light,
spoke the mouse, *to beckon*
Yet, this taper is not equal to the illumination of a firefly.

And is not this house
a signal, answered the second,
as she waved her lantern back and forth over the fields.
(Never in the days of her childhood had she handled a weapon).

Yes, continued the mouse, but the harvesting season comes.

(Towards the end of her life, she was forced to leave Athens.)

And we must move,
or become threshed.

She wept as she saw the number of the dead:

A lighthouse could summon all
from the sea of barley

She returns to the dream of no canopy.

A house which exists only in sleep.

She returns to the evening sky
of all rivers.

A robe of white water.

Her sorrowing chambers worn with entrances,
Complexion pink-ed in candle domain.

She flits between silences of paper as
all things belong to their moorings.

They followed one another to the house lost in sleep,

Borrowed footsteps proceed down the hall
she had none in her possession.

She refuses the only boat back.
A paper parasol forbids.

The first tier of solitude persists

In the middle
of her bed

a rivulet

The myth of the city suspended over her as she sleeps.

I need to get away from this highway, thought the ant while carrying a large boulder of bread.

(He imagines marching three times around the body of the dead queen, in his bronze equipment, she laid out in her tomb).

I do not wish to be a part of this empire. I am so tired of burying the dead.

The ant stepped away from the hill.

(He imagines a mass desertion, a wild rush for the city gates, as a flock of doves with a swift hawk after them).

I do not wish to turn back upon those steps I have taken out of such necessity, but remain within my furthest body, hoping that it may carry me furthest from my earlier forms.

But no one had the sense to note that they were landing on the very island they had left.

(He had heard an oracle summon with the promise: there remains a map of the sun within your eye).

She returns to her bed of clouds. Entering water to remember the future. Who will teach the house, she asks. *Don't worry, we'll hire a horse.* She buries the doll with corn silk hair. She takes a pine needle bath. Rocks and mosses furnish her home. A dowser crossed her path saying, I may go anywhere, there is water all over the world. She goes and digs up the dolls, to see if they're still dead.

Her fingers will not weep
within a ship's distance of herself,

Her hand upon the black beak,
disappearing.

Her amulet of leaves,
pear-shaped

green globes within water, pendulous
waiting to part   from their branches

With outstretched arms I could see her next home.

The birds act as if they belonged.

The dog found a fortune of thimbleberries belonging to a shepherdess who guarded the toads of the land. And where are your sheep, he ventured to ask. *They are happier lost.* And the toads? *The toads disappear when their land's misfortune is pressing.*

The daughter was found sobbing nearby, and was carried home in blankets to her bed where she remained for several days. When she had recovered she began to consider occupations, and yet since all possibilities seemed remote and unfounded she remained throughout her childhood years, a shepherdess of land, in secret, and with no confidantes.

Golden poppy whose flame emits sleep,
as slender cups and delicate stems.

A forest alchemy
To sleep upon fire

The house does not remain indoors
The way a match is hemmed through winter

As heavier than air machines have left the ground
As electricity was once thought to be fanciful

The Sleep of Lamps

What will come easily, less so than night, or manners. I walk whether wanting or ill laden. Place this question in your company. In what pasture will sleep pervade? What word is done with pleasure?

How many scoffed and went along their ways? Whose dress spread like a fan?

I have watched the black and white bee hide his body within a flower.

I have watched the out of doors move, and asked, *where are you going?*

A white feather beside a small knife and a bottle of scented water were placed carefully upon a mirror. As she stepped out into the courtyard, a flood of light.

Shoulders clasped and unclasped.

An everworrying chain of petaled eclipse.

From the first dream of dispossession she hid her eyes.

For wandering find a black powder. If all turns to dust find water. With water make a poultice to eyes.

Her name is not mentioned by roadside, or upon any body of water.

Her name is not a dark powder.

This is not a sound that can be made like rain.

A skeleton may follow her cup.

Within an arched doorway, a lisp.

In this way you may speak the drawn syllables, strung, clasped and held together by the ever thoughtful tides.

The last year of her childhood was coaxed, kept upon a birch shelf, and attended, placed between comb and mirror.

She had never seen her surroundings within borders. Darkened eyelids held a sound heard only in sleep.

Delivering lamps, a girlhood pastime.

And if you seek sound, plummet silence.

And if you seek illumination, set to delivering eyes.

Her tides set to tending the sleep of small villages.

In this way you may rest upon the floating mirror, and wander between doorways, unhinged afar.

A searching reference remains.
Eyes which act as catapults ignite a ship.

Fire was suspended where she pressed
her cheek against a stone wall.

She answers the letters made of mud

And delivers the excess light
 at the end of each season

a daughter rather like a white rabbit

As if a negative were to be placed underneath her skin.

She walks, a white letter by her side.

Having lived her entire livelihood without ever seeing a reflection of herself, when asked to draw what she imagined, she drew first a series of waves, and then a star.

If wood is made of light and air,
and motion made of light

days pass without weather, without whereabouts.

If days are made of wood and air.
If minds are made of whereabouts.

The house of paper is rescue.
the way a page is used as sky

The way weather is made of houses

And light is made of motion

Hands Made Of Mercury

"No life now wanders like an unfettered stream: there is a mill wheel for the tiniest rivulet to turn"

—Nathaniel Hawthorne

Last night we were good skeletons
carrying portions of porridge to cellar doors.

Riding a horse into uncharted danger, a storm upholds its privacy.

This uncharted night of cellar doors.
This mansion, sitting upon a horse.

Swindlers purloined treacherous fading passageways.

A daughter rather like a drawing room.

A crusade rather like a heap of stones.

A direct descendant of the red damask

The voice inside that machine is not to be removed no matter how urgently it may beg.

Please do not disturb the list of jobs.

All names are given to stand for legends.

I am writing this on the skin of my knee.

Ten, twenty-fifth avenues are waiting.

When I lived in the message house, the garden birds followed my research.

A type of incendiary intuition

I set the rose document on the broken branch.

Those pages of leaves will not yellow any further.

My seven lobed child set out the broken leaf.

My seven yellow sight.

I am of one-hundred and eight minds.

I press this leaf and then place it before me. I press the rose furniture into a book.

The Fountain's Lament:

As his tears fell into a fountain, a boy was startled when the fountain spoke, asking him to disappear.

The boy stood saying, *I thought sorrow must be parted.*

To be forsaken by a fountain is not common, but his tears contained more salt than would be expected, in each a small ocean. And so he left, taking his sorrow away, catching what salt he could upon a narrow leaf which did not complain.

The madame turned to limestone

Tales were told after meals
to the churners and kneaders
the voltage keepers and welders.

Their hearts were recalibrated as rain in a wheel

The dress master of the canary held her perched on a velvet cushion, while tailoring her frock.

She said, the music of that orchestra is very large, and so I must have a large cape.

This is the song the canary sung while flying over the evening party, with her new robes trailing below her.

Many pulled aside their masks to admire the spectacle.

The thief, her partner takes advantage while all heads are lifted in the dense crowd.

Again the calendar turns before I am certain the ladybug has left the page.

In Boltenia is a volted gate. A stairway of tumbling assets. In Boltenia I ate bread and became a voltage keeper. I borrowed from that book until I could borrow no longer.

The threadbare have no rustle.

A parlor door is known to shiver. When assaulted on all sides, a wishbone is no vouchsafe. Air in natural motion may vanish like a curtained soul.

If you think of work animals as oaken buckets.

I am told, you must construct the future with no scowl. This location appears to be possessed by the east wind. The length of one's brows will accomplish little.

Behind every clock, a somnambulist.

A gold tree against the gold afternoon. Everything else is the testimony of sparse omens.

A Girl in The Woods

*We hide in the woods to remember
the simultaneous noise of the city,
wearing the ring of the city.*

—Lee Ann Brown

The thorn hedge mirages are perishing

Dear launch accomplice, I am waiting.

A brief exodus on the avenue of horse chestnut trees. The centers have left the Chinese Paper. Burgundy leaf in a field of dross. I sleep in a skein of numbers. The atmosphere is rain. My November hangs from this little hook.

There is rain in a fleet of ships, *there is rain in my name.*

A lock of night is sequestered.

I found this book on a shelf that did not exist. A wall which was smooth and actual. This is the tantamount difficulty of starlets. They are ruined beyond a gazebo to search for that which appears to be marble, but turns to dust upon waking.

I dreamed of a bluebird in a satchel. Signs appeared in sequels, flaunting along the roadsides, tending corn. I may choke upon doves, their continuous thickets pliant languid coos.

Gold light from a mirror woke me.
The mirror disappeared and the light remained.

We have arrived beyond destiny's memory

    a paper umbrella my escort

                      A mutiny of solitude

a house of wind

My walls are moving curtains

    the chairs have blown away

Birds of paradise

    whose beaks

    I believed and later disbelieved this flower

Something had been tossed from my head

    A ghost-headdress

Her chin is tilted down. One arm is raised at eye level, on a diagonal. The other is at her hip.

>The resulting accident as if she were a pitcher.

Her legs are coincidental, no brushstrokes. As if they were no particular settings beneath her carriage.

>The dress is forest white, *flounced.*

The image contains no color.

Behind the card on which she stands is another identical image.

>from asphodels, and brookline, a misfortune of voices

>*She found the blank dream*

She was holding it to her chest with her chin, staggering for balance, and this was the pose.

My legs are pale lilies. When I lived here, in a draft house, the garden market followed my marriage. A carriage crystallized. Tracks of snails, lanterns, pool the leaves along a trail.

At the yellow hour, the nearest mountains are awake.

I sleep concealed in thickets

The unexpected lies an oar
This offering whispered on wood

I set out with the chinese money holding the staff in my fist. Fingers closed around the emblems, translucent as those worlds below. Ephemeral as dust, dandelion seed.

A staff with a clear torch is being handed down below the foliage.

Waving opal palettes. Each oculi, quill point on effervescent skin. Snail wrappings.

A mock tribe of sleeping beings. A paper vessel slips.

I send pressed maple, pressed oak, yellow others, red possibles. Press the slight breeze for opal dust.

Thus she becomes every character and will not delineate. This is not deduction, but suggestion, whereby the headpieces may be searched for, and later bargained upon.

At the scene of the auction:

The criminal sat on the ground bent over a headpiece. It was her headpiece, she had left it but a moment ago.

He asked, "have you by any chance seen a tiara covered with flowers?"

She answered, "the woods are filled with them" *gathering goldenrod, covering her head with the blooms.*

"The woods are filled with the mischief of the oaken hand, and thieves such as myself."

CRANE:

A seed remains within its chambers, just as an answer strays from your lips.

GIRL:

The ever blooming tides have said much the same, the quick following lights and lanterns, the roadsides and thickets.

The garden became a gateway, a threshold, a balcony stepping out onto air. The trellised vines. Wisteria trails.

A garden of air with such pull.

Surely then her orbit is disturbed, her sleeping and waking. Thoughts tend to wax and wane. She had considered the crane an imaginary eclipse of her senses.

Some entities require no door, nor doorstep, yet there still remains the question of threshold.

In order to return, she may cross over that pile of misgivings.

That you stop in my steps is not snow. The cards said travel. I follow the ends of my gown and the tablet of sketches we found from your childhood.

There is no agency but the wind itself. I walk and I alter in my footsteps. I looked down and placed her unshod foot over the invisible strings, which felt mildly like pearls, and stepped across to that neighborhood of streams I had so long ago visited.

Her figure in a clearing was set apart in a stance. A misfortune of voices staggering for balance set forth these brushstrokes. Earlier participants said:

She is in battlestance, or otherwise, with her
Hand outstretched, she tests the wind, or if not
Her arm at a diagonal, points towards the future.
She is summoning,
Or plays an invisible instrument, or
Strings a bow.
Otherwise, she unfurls a scroll, and if not
She is then dousing with a long pendant.

Said the crane, she is dressed for the part. That or some other dance.

A long visit with the pepper tree

Teeth stained black with antimony.

Asphodel and brookline spoke forth in acronyms.

The grasses speak:

What posture disjuncture begins borrowing?

Trees were torches which lit up the road

In an acorn boat between crags to reach the ceremony

She was expected in vertigo
between torches, the red grasses

A long visit with grasses in a small boat between acronyms

What posture disjuncture lit up the ceremony?

She set out within a field of flax, walking beyond her coat
where daylight catches and sears her skin.

She was sent to awaken a sleeping portrait
To decipher the speech of roses
She memorizes the smoke within a mirror

Walking beyond postures, which body reaches furthermore
first,

where accomplices carry the road?

I know not how I came upon this field of flax. The road carries me as a doll which does not speak. The hearing of the tree increases as the rain continues.

Still, like no clockwork.

No silent forms of persuasion could move the body out of mind where it dwelled. She stood exactly within her body as if she had only one body, so that her previous movements could not be traced in the air around her.

Statues even cannot complete this type of stillness since they have been mounted by quivering hands. They may shake in a rough wind. Whereas she stood as if there were no surroundings which could be called a separate interior.

Shall I compare her to a clock? With no hands, if hands can be defined by movement.

Being such, her limbs were rooted in the air, and her bare feet seemed to sink into the ground.

Being such, set apart like clockwork, she stood in silent forms of persuasion, within her interior. Bare feet as clauses, as is so often the case. Most trees could move the hands to think otherwise, but she traced the air around her with stillness.

Robes flowering make no sound, and I within them make no sound but a faint rustle.

The golding of leaves
    _____ lives in a raindrop

I place this emblem around my neck when all is sealed.

The estuary of night has carried away all buildings to wane within a bird's eye.

Gilt cages were worn as ornaments. Musical instruments were left to their own devices.

Desirable nowheres, being thus, a pose so held in concentration that none could pierce the quietness surrounding.

This is my rowing pasture.

She drinks one chance draught.
Here you may lay her gilt head.
In a pasture overgrown with ornaments.
Vials of quietness litter the ground.

To string lakes in search of polemics is a map
which may be tied around the chest for safekeeping.

She woke with a wooden sense of charm, rowing away from those sleeping grounds filled with tokens for those who may forget their way.

Her encoder ring held a small light needed to find the badge of leaves marked September, through a startled looking glass, crinkling. An aria having thought that light the moon.

For which lake I was navigating may be lost, as my glimpse of the coast is drowned as I open my eyes. I see the edge of a door or pattern of light. I wear this satchel as a badge of the woods, a flare as a lobster mushroom.

When meals or days are not well hung I will do as I wish. Follow a deer into distances, consume large piles of leaves. Walk amiably amidst shadow. Finishing a book in strange code, I glance ahead, uncertain of what has occurred.

Shadows on the tree trunks speak with such gravity.

I would follow this nectar guide, if I could be persuaded to be so small.

She was remembered as: the line of one dress which forms a bare outline; ceremonies before fruit trees; trimming of the early hours when mornings sit in leisure; red hair in winter light.

The day's tentacles have succumbed. I kneel to remain in the presence of daylight, asking what I have brought to the altar of afternoon.

Draw near a journey and pull up your horse

If you have no horse this means wait.

A thrush and a midnight watch over a shoulder.

I walk this way as a garden unbroken,

where we dig the same fortress.

Epilogue and Prologue

At the end of a series of portals she has the ability to recognize many disguises she has previously worn. Thus, many characters are strewn across her pond bed. It is quite an unsightly mess, and nonetheless, many of them escape each time she turns her head. This is the way she had planned the cessation of these misadventures. All disguises swim.

photo by Brad Davidson

Laynie Browne was born in 1966, and grew up in Los Angeles. She received a B.A. in English Literature from the University of California, Berkeley in 1988, and an M.F.A. from Brown University in 1990. With others, she curated the poetry series at the Ear Inn in New York City from 1992-1995. She received a fellowship from the MacDowell Colony in 1992, and was awarded the Gertrude Stein Award in Innovative American Poetry three times between 1993 and 1996. She lives in Seattle where she teaches poetry in public schools as a writer-in-residence, and is one of the curators of the Subtext Reading Series. Her other books are *Hereditary Zones*, Boog Literature (1993), *One Constellation* (Leave Books, 1994), *Rebecca Letters* (Kelsey St. Press, 1997) and *LORE* (Instress, 1998).